The London Lion Hunt

ISBN 978-1-908921- 02-4
Printed and bound in Great Britain by Hertfordshire Display plc

Acknowledgements
A very special thank you to Sam, for working his magic.

Thank you to all the people who have trialled the trail for us;
Natasha and Victoria Oates, Lorraine, Emily, Jennifer and Bethany Hooper,
Tracey, Ruby and Arun Soor and Phoebe Skinner.
Thanks also to Miranda and Duncan Brown, Charlotte Tizzard, Fanxin and Luiqi Fang,
Diane Donat, and many other friends and family members who have helped us.

Front cover pictures from top to bottom:
Trafalgar Square Lion in the afternoon sun
The Buxton Memorial in Victoria Tower Gardens
Richard the Lionheart, outside the Palace of Westminster

Back cover pictures from top to bottom:
The South Bank Lion
Bazalgette River Lions

The London Lion Hunt

For Nicholas Mark

A **step outside** Guide

CONTENTS

Travel Tips

- Travelcards give unrestricted travel on buses, trains and the Underground any time after 9.30am on weekdays, and all day at weekends.

- If you are travelling from outside the Travelcard area, ask at your station for the best way of including central London buses in your ticket (it may be cheapest to buy a bus ticket separately when you get to London).

- Tube maps are available free at every Underground station.

- The Transport for London website is www.tfl.gov.uk

INTRODUCTION

Welcome!

Welcome to this book, and welcome to London, splendid city of lions!

I am William the South Bank Lion, and I'm going to lead you on safari through the urban jungle to meet some of my lion friends. We're going to find out why they live in London, and how some of them got here.

We will be right in the heart of the capital, surrounded by some of the finest buildings in the world.

We are going to take the day at a stately pace, to give us time to absorb and enjoy everything - I've reserved good picnic and resting places for us for when our feet (and paws) get a little weary.

Pages six and seven will tell you everything you need to know to prepare for the day, and then we are ready for the London Lion Hunt to begin.

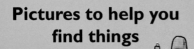

How to use your book

Pictures to help you find things

Good picnic spots

Accessibility information for buggies and wheelchairs

Free toilets

Lion Alert!

One of my lion friends is nearby!

Tick the pawprint when you have seen him

What to wear or bring with you

Comfortable shoes

Your picnic

Pencils and pens for *Rest your legs* pages

Your camera

Binoculars if you have some

Clothes and extras that suit the weather

IMPORTANT SAFETY INFORMATION!

● Remember that London is very big and very busy; drivers can be fast and impatient.

● Only cross the road at traffic lights or pedestrian crossings.

● Make sure your group stays close together - no-one wants to get lost!

Roadworks

If there are roadworks or building repairs there may be a diversion. Just take this as part of London life, and enjoy the detours. You may even discover something wonderful. If you do, then let us know at
www.stepoutsideguides.com

Useful information and accessibility

St Margaret's Church
Open **Mon - Fri** 9.30am - 3.30pm
Sat 9.30am - 1.30pm, **Sun** 2.00pm
- 5.00pm *www.westminster-abbey.org*
Wheelchair access is through the
North Door. Ask the Verger on

duty for help, or phone
020 7654 4840
beforehand.
May be closed
occasionally for special services.

National Portrait Gallery
Open daily 10.00am - 6.00pm
www.npg.org.uk

The first gallery
entrance is step-free
and leads through the
shop to a lift.

Horse Guards Parade
The horse guard changes every hour
on the hour from 10.00am - 4.00pm

Tube: There is a lift to the street
at Westminster Station. Turn left

out of the lift and you
are facing Westmin-
ster Bridge. There is
no step-free access at
Leicester Square Station.

Buses: There is no step-free
access at Leicester Square
Station, but the 24 bus, from
stop J on Charing Cross Road,
goes back to Westminster
Station. All buses can
accommodate wheelchairs
except for the old Routemasters.

READY, STEADY, GO!

Starting Point:
Westminster Station: Circle, **District** & Jubilee Lines

Finishing Point:
Leicester Square Station: **Piccadilly & Northern** Lines

Walking distance: about 5km, 3.1 miles.
Time: About five hours at a leisurely pace, with breaks.

Leave the station by exit 1. Turn right and go up the steps and you'll see Big Ben straight ahead of you. What a spectacular start to the day!

We'll be seeing more of Big Ben later, but for now, turn left and cross over the river on Westminster Bridge. There's a great view across and along the Thames.

The London Eye has more visitors each year than the Taj Mahal or the Pyramids in Egypt.

There are toilets in the ticket hall of the London Eye.

On the South Bank you can see the HUGE wheel of the London Eye. Watch it for exactly one minute; can you see it slowly turning? It takes half an hour to go right round once.

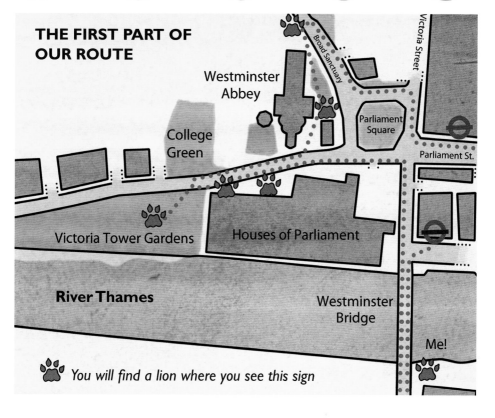

THE FIRST PART OF OUR ROUTE

Westminster Abbey

College Green

Parliament Square

Broad Sanctuary

Victoria Street

Parliament St.

Victoria Tower Gardens

Houses of Parliament

River Thames

Westminster Bridge

Me!

🐾 *You will find a lion where you see this sign*

THE LONDON EYE; SOME IMPRESSIVE NUMBERS!

How high?
135m
How heavy?
Over 2,000 tonnes

How many capsules?
Count them!
People per capsule?
Up to 25

So, how many people can ride at a time?
Work it out!

Answers on page 32

PLEASED TO MEET YOU!

I **am at the end of the bridge. Keep going and you will soon find me.**

I stand here, on my high **plinth** looking out over the Thames. I have watched the river go by since 1837, but not always from this spot.

The plaque on the far side of the plinth, tells you all about where I started life. It will give you the answers to the questions to fill in on this page.

When I was new, I was painted bright red!

Now I can join you for the rest of the day! Let's walk on to the traffic lights, about 50 metres away. Cross over the road so that we can walk back on the other side of Westminster Bridge.

The South Bank Lion

Where did I live when I was first made?

....

Why was I moved?

....

Who asked for me to be moved? (Ahem, what an honour…)

....

Do you think I look fierce or friendly?

....

Answers on page 32

Just as you start to cross the river, look along the river bank on our left. Can you see a row of lion heads with rings in their mouths?

The Bazalgette Lions were put in place when the Albert Embankment (the 'wall' of the river) was built by Joseph Bazalgette in the 1860s. It is said that 'when the lions drink, London will sink'. How big is the gap between the water and the lions' mouths? Nowadays there is very little danger of London flooding because the Thames Barrier protects the City.

Did you remember to tick the paw prints?

From this bridge we get one of the very best views of the magnificent Houses of Parliament. It looks even more beautiful in the sunshine. Are we lucky with the weather today?

If you look carefully, you can see the **terrace** with striped **awning**, facing the river, where Members of Parliament (MPs) and members of the House of Lords can sit and have their lunch.

The MPs sit under the green awning ...

... and the Lords and Ladies sit under the red.

THE PALACE OF WESTMINSTER

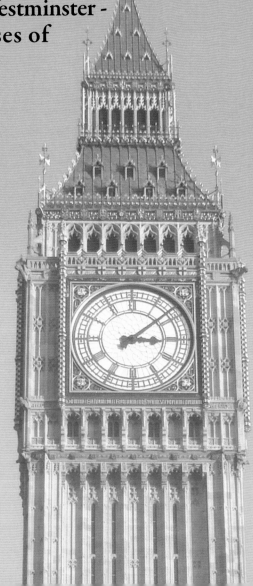

We're going to walk right up to the Palace of Westminster - usually called the Houses of Parliament - and past Big Ben now.

I was made in exactly the same year the Palace of Westminster was built - 1837.

✦

Everyone calls this clock Big Ben, but that is really the name of the biggest bell, up at the top of the tower. The whole clock is the Great Westminster Clock, and the tower is the Elizabeth Tower.

✦

Did you know that a clock CHIMES when it plays a tune, and STRIKES when it bongs the hour?

✦

I love hearing Big Ben ringing out across the river at night. It must be VERY loud inside the tower!

✦

Now let's turn the corner, still keeping Parliament to our left. Walk for about 100 lion paces until you see a statue of a man on a plinth, on the grass to our left.

Can you see who he is?

 My friend Edmund the lion is at the base of the plinth, guarding Cromwell.

Why is Oliver Cromwell in front of the Houses of Parliament? Read the box below to find out.

Members of Parliament (MPs) are elected at each **General Election** to speak for the people who voted for them. Their duties include making laws and discussing topics that are important to all of us - like health, education, the environment and transport.

Roundhead helmet

Cavalier hat

Oliver Cromwell
(1599 – 1658)

Until 1642 kings and queens ruled England and their word was law. Some people (the Roundheads) disagreed with this, and led by Cromwell they went to war against those who supported the King (the Cavaliers). This was the English Civil War. The Roundheads won, King Charles I was beheaded, and ever since our laws have been made by Parliament. We still have a queen (or king) but they don't make laws.

So Cromwell is a hero of Parliament but he was, and still is, a **controversial** figure.

PARLIAMENTARY LIONS

Now we walk on to the end of the Houses of Parliament.

How many lions can you see carved into the stonework of the building?

Some are hard to spot. Just after St Stephen's Tower, is Old Palace Yard, which is used as a car park. Sometimes you can see Government Ministers arriving in their big black cars. In the middle of the Yard is a large statue of our next lion. Can you see him?

It's a trick! The statue is of a soldier on a horse, sword held high, riding to battle! He is King Richard I, known as Richard the Lionheart, so I have included him in our lion hunt.

He does look splendid, though not as splendid as a real lion.

Playing hoopla with Richard the Lionheart.

Richard the Lionheart reigned from 1189-1199 and was a warrior king. He led a Crusade and fought wars in Europe but spent very little time in England, and *probably couldn't even speak English!* However, he has held his place in English tradition as one of the country's greatest rulers.

The last doorway we pass is the Sovereign's Entrance. Can you see a lion standing each side of the archway, holding a flag? They don't look like real lions, but the sort that are used on coats of arms; these are called Heraldic Lions.

Just past the Houses of Parliament we come to Victoria Tower Gardens and this is a very good place to take a break.

Rest-your-legs page

There are interesting things to see
in Victoria Tower Gardens, so let's rest our legs here for a while
before we explore.

The large group statue is called 'The Burghers of Calais'. Read the plaque
to find out why Rodin, the artist, created it. Can you see how big the
Burgher's hands and feet are? Now, can you draw a picture of the people
in your group, and give them BIG hands and feet? You could include me.
Here's a picture for you to copy.

SPITTING LIONS

Up towards the other end of the gardens there is a very fancy shelter. Let's go and see what it is.

It's the Buxton Memorial, which is a fountain built in 1834 to honour a group of men who worked to end slavery. In 2007 it was restored to its original grandeur to celebrate the 200th anniversary of the end of the slave trade.

Can you see that the water spouts are lion heads? So, here are my spitting lions, but sadly they no longer do their work as the fountain doesn't supply water (it is an 'ex-fountain'.) Now run across to the river

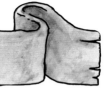

wall. As you look across the river, you can see our Bazalgette Lions. There are loads of them – even I don't know how many!

It is time to leave the gardens now, using the gate where we came in.

Near the gate is a statue of Emmeline Pankhurst. This inspiring woman led the Suffragette movement, which campaigned for women to have the right to vote for their MPs in the same way that men did. Their aim was finally achieved in 1928.

Votes for women!

Turn right and cross the road on the first crossing. To our left is College Green.

If a Member of Parliament is interviewed on the news, they are often standing on College Green, with Big Ben behind them.

St Margaret's Church:
Opening times:
Mon-Fri 9.30am - 3.30pm
Saturdays 9.30am -1.30pm
Sundays 2.00pm - 5.00pm
Wheelchair access is through the North door.
Ask the verger on duty for assistance.

With our backs to the Green, we are going to walk past one end of Westminster Abbey.
Immediately after we've passed the Abbey, we turn left, through the black gate.
Westminster Abbey is now on our left. On our right is a smaller church, St Margaret's. There are a few lions living there and we're going to visit them now!

St Margaret's Church is about 500 years old, and it is a beautiful building, lit with brass **candelabras**.

Westminster Abbey

Kings and Queens have been crowned on this holy ground since 1066. The beautiful church you see today, facing the Houses of Parliament, was built from 1245. Prince William and Kate Middleton were married here in April 2011.

THE LIONS OF SAINT MARGARET'S

We enter the church at the back. Near the front on the right is a tomb, with a lion lying at the feet of the statues.

Can you find him? I feel sorry for my noble friend – he has a very boring job. I visit him sometimes, and tell him what is going on in the lion world.

Look at the elaborate tombs around the walls of the church. I think they are amazing.

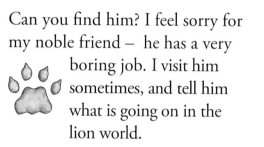

There are three more lions, at the base of the **lectern**. Can you find them?

Remember that this is a place of worship for Christians; please be respectful. No running or roaring!

REMEMBERING SOLDIERS

As we come out of St Margaret's Church a grassy area faces us.

Each November, this is transformed into a 'Garden of **Remembrance**' where relatives of soldiers who have died in war place a poppy on a cross in memory of their loved ones.

We're going to walk to the far end of this lawn to find some more lions. At the end of the Abbey, on the wide pavement, a large column commemorates the past pupils of Westminster School who died in wars in the 1800s. Can you  see the lions on it?

Now we need to return to Parliament Square.

Follow this map closely, as street names change every few metres. Cross to Parliament Street (which will become Whitehall).

We're going to walk to Trafalgar Square from here.

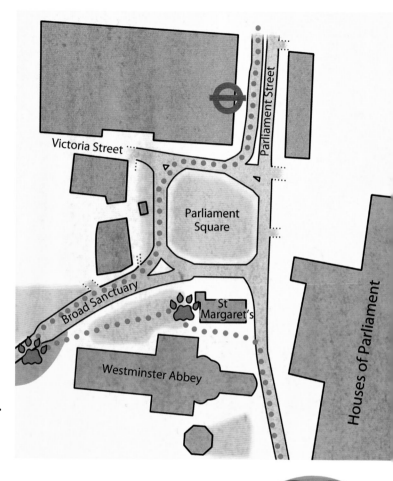

Parliament Street

Victoria Street

Parliament Square

Broad Sanctuary

St Margaret's

Westminster Abbey

Houses of Parliament

If you prefer you can catch a bus along Whitehall, all of them go to Trafalgar Square.
The map shows the bus stop. You will see the most interesting sights best if you sit on the left hand side of the bus.

There are lots of traditional phone boxes around here. How many can you spot?

WHITEHALL

Whitehall is a VERY important road, lined with Government buildings. Which of these can you spot as we walk along?

Foreign Office ☐
Ministry of Defence ☐
Treasury ☐
Cabinet Office ☐
Scottish Office ☐

Downing Street

The Prime Minister lives at Number 10 Downing Street. I wish you could go right up to the door and see the splendid lion knocker!

← Parliament Sq.
PARLIAMENT ST.

The Cenotaph is the memorial to every British soldier who has lost their life in war. Cenotaph is Greek, and means 'empty tomb'. The Remembrance Day service which the Queen attends is held here every year.

PARLIAMEN
STREET SW
←
CITY OF

Can you fi

Each of the iron bollards along the pavement on Whitehall carri

Some of my friends live here - real horses, who stand on sentry duty with their soldier.
The soldiers, from the Household Cavalry, have impressive uniforms and VERY shiny boots, but I like the horses best!

This WWII memorial is dedicated to the seven million British women who contributed to the war effort.

Horse Guards Parade

Trafalgar Sq. →

WHITEHALL

WHITEHALL
W1
→

STER

roadsign?

You will see the Royal Coat of Arms on a lot of buildings here.
It is used by the Government as a symbol of the United Kingdom. Of course the Queen herself uses it too! The Royal Coat of Arms has a lion to represent England, and a Unicorn to represent Scotland.

crest of Westminster City, with two lions holding it up.

TRAFALGAR SQUARE

At the end of Whitehall we arrive in Trafalgar **Square.**

Those of you on the bus, listen for the announcement.
We all need to cross the road (on the crossing.) to Nelson's Column. You can't miss it!

At the base of the Column lie four of the most magnificent lions in the whole of London. They are also some of the most famous lions in the world! Even while they were being made, they were famous.

These lions were created by Edwin Landseer in 1867

I like to make sure all the lions look their best.

In a gallery close by, there is a painting of the lions being made - we'll see that later.

Rest-your-legs page

Trafalgar Square is an excellent place to take a
break, and watch London life go by.
People from all over the world come here,
speaking many different languages!

LION CROSSWORD

Clues across: 3. To go exploring in lion country. **5.** A group of lions,
and how I feel to be in it. **7.** A wardrobe, a witch and this lion!
Clues down: 1. The most important part of my fur. **2.** A little lion noise!
4. A female lion. **5.** My feet, when I stop. **6.** A big lion noise!

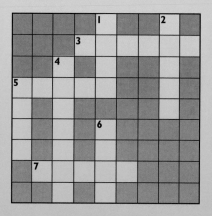

Answers: **3** SAFARI, **5** PRIDE, **7** ASLAN, **1** MANE, **2** GROWL, **4** LIONESS, **5** PAWS, **6** ROAR

Lion laughter - Jolly jokes

Match up the questions and the answers!

• Do lions cook their dinner? • How's the lion hunt going?
• Why can you see lions in pairs here? • How often do lions eat people?
• Who do lions dress-up as at Christmas?

• No they eat roar meat! • Every chewsday! • Santa Claws!
• SAFARI, so goody! • There are double yellow lions on every street!

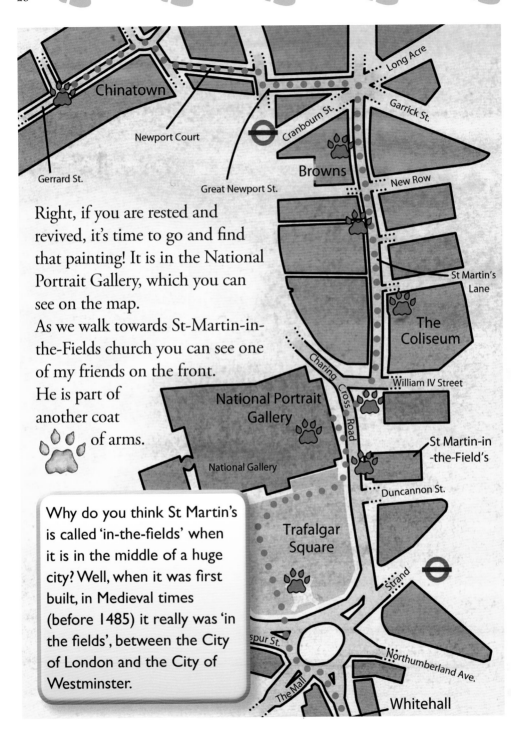

Chinatown

Newport Court

Long Acre

Garrick St.

Cranbourn St.

Browns

New Row

Gerrard St.

Great Newport St.

St Martin's Lane

Right, if you are rested and revived, it's time to go and find that painting! It is in the National Portrait Gallery, which you can see on the map.

As we walk towards St-Martin-in-the-Fields church you can see one of my friends on the front.

He is part of another coat of arms.

The Coliseum

William IV Street

National Portrait Gallery

National Gallery

Charing Cross Road

St Martin-in-the-Field's

Duncannon St.

Why do you think St Martin's is called 'in-the-fields' when it is in the middle of a huge city? Well, when it was first built, in Medieval times (before 1485) it really was 'in the fields', between the City of London and the City of Westminster.

Trafalgar Square

Strand

spur St.

Northumberland Ave.

The Mall

Whitehall

A PORTRAIT OF LIONS

Here we are at the main gallery entrance (see map). It has a revolving door, which is a bit of a squeeze for a lion - but I like it anyway.

National Portrait Gallery
The first gallery entrance is step-free and leads through the shop to a lift.

Can you spot these things in the lion picture?

Dog ☐
Basket ☐
Lion skin ☐
Measuring instrument ☐
Drawing of a lion ☐
Painting ☐
Knife ☐
Bucket ☐

Go straight up the stairs ahead of you, then turn and continue up two more flights to the first floor. Turn right immediately – can you see the rows of black **busts** on shelves?
Walk up to them, then turn left through the doorway into room 24, and the painting is facing us.
Don't the lions look splendid!

John Ballantyne painted this picture in 1865. People thought it was a portrait of Edwin Landseer, creating the lions. We know better of course - it is a portrait of these fabulous lions, being prepared to take their place in Trafalgar Square!

As we leave the gallery, using the same entrance/exit, there is a statue of a lady across the road from us. Let's go and have a look at it – and find another lion. The lady's name is Edith Cavell.

And the lion? We'll find him at the back of the statue. He's a big lion, carved in **bas relief** - grubby, too, poor thing and needing a good clean!

Edith Cavell was a nurse who was killed by the Germans for saving allied soldiers (they were the soldiers who fought with the British) in Belgium in World War I. The inscription gives the words she spoke the evening before she died, and these show us just what a special person she was. Can you see them?

'Patriotism is not enough. I must have no hatred or bitterness for anyone'

FORTITUDE

The lion represents 'Fortitude' which is the quality of bearing pain, bad luck and great difficulties (and perhaps being left dirty for a long time) without complaining, but just 'getting on with it'.

We are going to walk down St Martin's Lane now.

LIONS HIGH AND LOW

There are all sorts of lions to find along here, up high and down low, then we'll finish our day meeting two rather special lions from far, far away.

Right at the top of the Coliseum is a slowly revolving globe; watch it carefully to see it move.

At the top of the Chandos pub on the corner of St Martin's Lane is a brewer, shifting his barrel of beer around. I hope he doesn't drop it!

Just along from the Chandos is a very grand opera house, called The Coliseum, and up on the roof are four terracotta lions, looking right out across London.

this lovely sign hanging out over the pavement? Opposite it is a row of shops with a lion head over each large window. They aren't very big, so you'll have to look carefully, but they

We'll see them clearly in a minute. As you look down the road, can you see

are rather nice. Turn round at this point for a good view of the lions and the globe on the Coliseum.

Just along from these shops is Brown's Restaurant, with a Royal Coat of Arms over the door. Do you think the Queen eats her dinner here? (I don't think so.) This building was once a County Court, and like all courtrooms, it displayed the Royal Coat of Arms to show that it was upholding the law of the land.

NEWPORT COURT WC2
新 港 圍
CITY OF WESTMINSTER 西敏市

At the junction, turn down the second road from the left, Great Newport Street, (see map p26). Cross Charing Cross Road into Newport Court, opposite. The road sign gives us a clue about our last two lions. Turn right at the end, then left, and here we are in Gerrard Street, the heart of London's Chinatown.

Chinatown

I love Chinatown; it is filled with wonderful sights, sounds and smells. Chinese people from all over London and even further away come here to buy food, meet friends and eat. If it is festival time, there may be hundreds of red paper lanterns strung across the street.

Halfway along the street, we meet my Chinese friends. They were a present to London Chinatown from China. They look different from the other lions we've met today. Do you think their roar would sound different too?

When you've finished exploring it's time for me to escort you to Leicester Square station. We're leaving Gerrard Street where we came in. Turn right, pass Newport Court, then as we turn left in to Little Newport Street there's the station, straight ahead.

I hope you've enjoyed our day. There are LOADS more lions in London, so when you're here, keep a look out and give them a wave! For now it's time for my friends and me to say...

'Goodbye and be happy' 再见，幸運

GLOSSARY & MORE LION IDEAS

GLOSSARY

p10 Plinth – the base that a statue stands on.

p11 Awning – A roof of cloth or plastic that covers an open space.

p11 Terrace – A level paved area outside a building.

p13 Controversial – Something is controversial when people argue about whether it is/was right or wrong.

p13 General Election – An election in which MPs are chosen at the same time for every area of the country.

p18 Candelabra – A large branched candle-stick or holder for several candles or lamps.

p19 Lectern – The bookstand at the front of the church, often in the shape of an eagle, on which the Bible is placed.

p20 Remembrance – The act of remembering.

p27 Bust – A statue of just the head and shoulders, and perhaps the chest.

p28 Bas relief – A shallow sculpture which just sticks out from the stone it is carved from.

More London Lions

To see more lions in London, visit the **British Museum**. There are lions on and beside the entrance door and once you're inside they are everywhere! There are statues from around the world, lions on plates, mosaic lions, lion wall plaques, lion door decorations and more.

The 2,500 year old Great Nineveh Lion Hunt frieze in room 10 tells the story of an ancient lion hunt in beautiful, though gory detail. It is one of the most wonderful lion treasures in the whole of London.

Answers

p9 There are 32 capsules. The London Eye holds up to 800 people at a time **p10** *I started life over the entrance of the Big Lion Brewery. The Brewery was bombed in WWII, King George VI asked for me to be moved.*

We hope you have enjoyed your day in London with your **Step Outside Guide!**
Let us know what you got up to. Leave a message at
feedback@stepoutsideguides.com
You can send pictures of your day to our online gallery @
gallery@stepoutsideguides.com